# WHAT ABOUT DEATH?

Mark T. Barclay

All scripture references are quoted from the
*King James Version* of the Holy Bible
unless otherwise noted.

Second Edition
First Printing 1997


ISBN 0-944802-21-4

Write:
Mark Barclay Ministries
P.O. Box 588, Midland, MI 48640-0588

# CONTENTS

# DEDICATION

"Earth is the only hell a 'Christian' will ever know! Earth is the only Heaven a 'sinner' will ever know."

— Dr. Roy Hicks Sr.

Imagine—a Christian's hell is a sinner's Heaven.

This is the worst it gets for you, Christian. It's the best it gets for sinners.

# A WORD FROM THE AUTHOR

I have seen and felt many people lose their loved ones to death. I have watched people in their sorrow, grief, and pity. I have seen them in funeral parlors and in the chapels with their eyes all red and their faces wrinkled with pain. I have seen so many who just couldn't comprehend the death of a loved one.

We live in a day when rock stars are dying of drug abuse and our young people are killing themselves because they claim they can't live without them.

Families go on filled with grief and pity; some actually lose their minds trying to hide from the reality of death.

I pray that this little book will set some of those people free and that it will shine some light on this subject of death. I pray you will read it with understanding, carefully studying the Scriptures.

I can recognize death as it comes. I met it as a young child when it took my father, and I met it again in the combat zone of Vietnam. I know it can defeat, but I also know it can be defeated!

# CHAPTER 1
# GOD'S THOUGHTS ON OUR ENEMY, DEATH

*"For my thoughts are not your thoughts, neither are your ways my ways, saith the LORD.*

*For as the heavens are higher than the earth, so are my ways higher than your ways, and my thoughts than your thoughts."*

Isaiah 55:8-9

It's time we live the Scriptures and take them seriously. God means what He gives us in His Word. God means it when He tells us that His thoughts and ways are higher than our thoughts and ways. I don't know about you, friend, but I want the thoughts of God on the Bible. I want the thoughts of God on this subject of death. My thoughts don't even count when they are different than God's thoughts. As I study the Bible, I find that my thoughts on death are so different than the thoughts of God. How about you?

*"Forasmuch then as the children are partakers of flesh and blood, he also himself likewise took part of the same; that through death he might destroy him that had the power of death, that is, the devil;*

1

*And deliver them who through fear of death were all
their lifetime subject to bondage."*
Hebrews 2:14-15

Are you afraid to die? Are you afraid to lose those
whom you love? Are you afraid of the dark, water, or air-
planes because you might lose your life? Here in Hebrews,
chapter 2, we see that many are **subject to bondage** all
their life because they are afraid of death.

*"But is now made manifest by the appearing of our
Saviour Jesus Christ, who hath abolished death, and
hath brought life and immortality to light through the
gospel . . ."*
2 Timothy 1:10

This scripture is so good! It tells us that we do not
need man's philosophy on this subject any longer. This
scripture tells us that Christ has abolished death and
brought life. Glory to God! We do not need to guess any
longer. We do not need to be in the dark about this any
longer. Praise God, He has brought life! This, of course,
doesn't mean that we will not die in the natural. It does
mean that we do not have to die in the supernatural. We do
not have to die spiritually. This scripture shows us life and
immortality **enlightened** through the gospel. You see, this
means we don't have to be in the dark any longer. We have
the answers in Christ; they are in the Bible.

*"For all our days are passed away in thy wrath: we
spend our years as a tale that is told.*

*The days of our years are threescore years and ten;
and if by reason of strength they be fourscore years,
yet is their strength labour and sorrow; for it is soon
cut off, and we fly away."*
Psalm 90:9-10

Many fight and strive to live here on this earth for at least 70 years. They believe that this is the ultimate! No, No, No! This scripture does tell us that the days of our years are 70 years and if we have enough strength we'll make it to 80. This is good, but let's look some more.

It also says that we spend our years "as a tale that is told." It says, "yet is their strength labour and sorrow; for it is soon cut off, and we fly away!" Now please understand what I am saying here. To go for 70 years is great, and the Bible does say that we should. But it is not the ultimate! To claim and believe to live this long is great, but it is not the ultimate!

*"The last enemy that shall be destroyed is death."*

1 Corinthians 15:26

It is true that death is not of God. It is an enemy. Jesus came to give us **life**, not death. It is the enemy who steals, kills, and destroys. Jesus wants us to have a totally abundant life. Here in 1 Corinthians 15:26, we see that death is the last enemy to be destroyed. However, we also need to see what God is telling us in verses 55-56 of this same chapter.

*"O death, where is thy sting? O grave, where is thy victory?*

*The sting of death is sin; and the strength of sin is the law."*

1 Corinthians 15:55-56

Death is an enemy, but the Bible says it is appointed unto us once to die. Should we fear? No. God always gives us the victory. We are to die once in the natural but not in the spiritual. We have eternal life. The Bible tells us that death has no sting—no sting! It doesn't hurt! The grave has no victory —no victory! If the Word of God says it, don't you think we should rest in it? We can die without giving the grave (enemy) or death (enemy) any victory.

Notice what verse 56 said: "The sting of death is sin . . ." We can interpret this two ways. To the sinner (those not born again) death has a horrible sting. When a family loses a loved one and they have no assurance where that loved one went or what is happening to them, this is sting—horrible sting.

# CHAPTER 2
# MY TESTIMONY

I remember as a 10-year-old boy my father dying. I remember looking into the casket to see his body absent of life. I looked with anticipation that he would move an arm or wink an eyelid, but there was nothing—absolutely no life. Nothing. My father was dead. Now let me tell you that as a 10-year-old boy who didn't really know Jesus, this was a horrible experience. I didn't understand it. I couldn't comprehend it. I couldn't find any peace at all. I was sick and tormented on the inside. I was angry at the world, my family, and even God.

I loved my father. I ran home from the funeral parlor that day yelling and screaming. A horrible hatred entered my heart. I turned against everyone. I ran upstairs in our old two-story home, I slammed my bedroom door behind me, and I yelled and screamed and hated and blamed everyone. I took furniture and placed it against the door so no one could enter. My mother and three brothers tried to reach me. I hated! Eventually, I came out of that room but not out of the bitterness and hatred. From that point I started living a tormented, terrible life.

I remember seeking relief through alcohol and fist fighting. When I would see another boy playing ball or having fun with his dad, I hated him. I would come home and beat on the walls of our garage. I remember hitting those old walls until I punched holes in them and my knuckles would bleed. Listen to this: I went to a friend's house one night to eat supper and spend the night. (I believe I was about 15 then.) He had such nice toys, he had a new bike and a nice football—and a super dad.

From that day I hated him. A few days later I caught him after school and beat him as bad as I could. Oh no, I'm not proud of this. I'm not bragging about this horrible state I was in, but many need to hear this. I refused to let go of my father who had died. I refused to let go; I refused to accept it. I chose to believe otherwise. Oh, there is such a horrible sting to death when you are not born again.

Now you see, my mother loved me tremendously. She still does. She did a very good job of being both a mother and father to four boys. But to me it didn't matter. I was hurt, bitter, and full of hate. You see, I used to think that if God was such a mighty God, then He could bring back my dad.

As I grew up, I realized it was selfish for me to desire my father back. The Lord showed me a vision (actually brought to my remembrance) of the day I was standing next to my father's casket. His preacher friend was standing there next to me. I began to cry, and he voiced to me that he knew my father well. He put his arm around me, and he told me that Dad was in good hands.

He shared with me how Dad loved me and how this death was not the fault of Dad or God. Through all those years of hatred and bitterness, I had forgotten that. As the Lord showed me this, my heart filled with joy. I realized it was my own selfish motives that wanted my father back. I asked the Lord for forgiveness and truly received it. Compassion and great appreciation flooded my soul for my mother. I so understood how hard it must have been for her.

I saw for the first time that for my dad to come back would only be to face death again. Where is he now? He is free from sin, sickness, and torment. Oh thank you, Jesus, for the truth sets us free.

Yes, friend, there is a horrible sting to death when we don't know Jesus as our personal Savior. Yes, there is a horrible sting to death when we don't know where our loved ones have gone. "The sting of death is sin." Now don't be fooled, believers can also put sting into death if they are not careful.

To the believer (born-again person) the sting of death is still sin. You see, we believers are supposed to know the Bible. We know where our deceased loved ones are, and we know what is happening to them.

For us to make a big, drawn-out, morbid, and painful ceremony in response to the death of a believer is putting sin or sting back into death. This is unscriptural. As we continue this study, you will see that to be absent from the body is to be present with the Lord—if you are born again (2 Cor. 5:8). Notice it says, "We are confident . . . and willing rather to be absent from the body, and to be present with the Lord." It is good to live here in this life, but your true citizenship is in Heaven if you are born again.

Live as long as you can, and pray for others to live long. But when they go, release them to Jesus. Yes, I believe in raising the dead. When God tells us specifically (rhema) to raise someone, we had better put our faith on it and obey immediately. But if He doesn't—relax!

> *"For to me to live is Christ, and to die is gain.*
>
> *But if I live in the flesh, this is the fruit of my labour:*
> *yet what I shall choose I wot not.*
>
> *For I am in a strait betwixt two, having a desire to*
> *depart, and to be with Christ; which is far better . . ."*
>
> Philippians 1:21-23

Wow! "For me to live is Christ, and to die is gain." Brother Barclay, do you mean to tell me that to die is to gain? Yes, yes, yes, if you are born again. Now remember, this isn't Barclay theology but rather Bible doctrine. We just read it all together. The Bible says it's gain. It's gain! It's gain! Now look here in verse 23. "For I am in a strait betwixt two . . ." In other words, Paul is saying that he is kind of caught between two decisions.

He knows he can do good for Christ if he stays, but he also shows us that it is his desire to be with his Lord. Notice also that in verse 23 Paul tells us that it is far better to be with Christ than to be in the world. Besides this, friends, Jesus is coming soon, and we should be preparing ourselves for His coming (our going), not for our staying. It is harvesttime, not seedtime.

# CHAPTER 3
# LAZARUS AND THE RICH MAN

*"There was a certain rich man, which was clothed in purple and fine linen, and fared sumptuously every day:*

*And there was a certain beggar named Lazarus, which was laid at his gate full of sores.*

*And desiring to be fed with the crumbs which fell from the rich man's table: moreover the dogs came and licked his sores.*

*And it came to pass, that the beggar died, and was carried by the angels into Abraham's bosom: the rich man also died, and was buried;.*

*And in hell he lift up his eyes, being in torments, and seeth Abraham afar off, and Lazarus in his bosom.*

*And he cried and said, Father Abraham, have mercy on me, and send Lazarus, that he may dip the tip of his finger in water, and cool my tongue; for I am tormented in this flame.*

*But Abraham said, son, remember that thou in thy lifetime receivedst good things, and likewise Lazarus evil things: but now he is comforted, and thou art tormented.*

*And beside all this, between us and you there is a great gulf fixed: so that they which would pass from hence to you cannot; neither can they pass to us, that would come from thence.*

*Then he said, I pray thee therefore, father, that thou wouldest send him to my father's house:*

*For I have five brethren; that he may testify unto them, lest they also come into this place of torment.*

*Abraham saith unto him, They have Moses and the prophets; let them hear them.*

*And he said, Nay, father Abraham: but if one went unto them from the dead, they will repent.*

*And he said unto him, If they hear not Moses and the prophets, neither will they be persuaded, though one rose from the dead."*

Luke 16:19-31

Here is what some call the parable of Lazarus and the rich man. However, I really don't believe Jesus is telling us a parable here but rather an account of a true incident. Either way, the impact and interpretation should be the same. We must also realize that Jesus is not teaching here to make a distinction between rich men and poor men only.

It is, however, good to understand that in that day rich people were considered good society for Heaven and poor people were all ungodly beggars. Thank God this was not and is not true with Jesus. He is a respecter of NO person. Look with me at verse 22. Here it says that the beggar was carried away by angels to Abraham's bosom, which is paradise. Now the rich man was buried, and we find him in verse 23 looking from hell. Remember now that this was before Jesus went into the lower parts of the earth for three days and three nights. It was called Hades.

Abraham's bosom was on one side; hell was on the other. A great gulf separated the two of them, and captive spirits of men were on each side but could not go from one side to the other. We see though that they could look and converse from one side to the other. Now hell hasn't changed much; there are still captive spirits of men that reside there, and they still thirst, and there are still wailings and gnashings of teeth. If you'll remember, Jesus led captivity captive; that is, He led the captive saints in Hades to the Father with Him.

Now (in this day) when we are absent from the body we are actually present with the Lord. We don't go to Abraham's bosom but rather to Jesus.

As a pastor, I have found that some people will believe anything that is told them. The basic person will not seek out a subject to find the actual truth. They would rather take the word of someone else, even if it isn't scriptural or proven to them with the Bible. Some people believe in purgatory. They believe that you sit in fire until someone buys you out or you burn your worth of sin away. If you sinned bad, you sit in hot fire a long time. If you sinned medium, you sit in medium fire for a medium amount of time, etc. This cannot be found in the Bible—anywhere.

Some people believe in soul sleeping. They think people just go to sleep and feel nothing, see nothing, and hear nothing until some great day of restitution.

Others believe in the totally dead theory. (By the way, these are all theories. They cannot be found in the Scriptures.) Remember now that we want God's thoughts on the subject. The totally dead theory makes us like a dog. While we are alive we are okay, but when we die, that is all there is to it—there is no God, no Heaven, no hell; you just roll over in a ditch and die. These people believe they will have no memory or feelings but rather cease to exist.

Listen friend, when you and I die, we are either going to be with Christ or the devil—Heaven or hell. A man once told me that he didn't believe in Heaven or hell. I explained to him that he wasn't wise. This is what I told him: "For me to live well on this earth as a Christian has cost me nothing; it has only improved my life. I have no medical bills, no ulcers, no hangovers. I am addicted to no drugs, I am happily married, and I feel great mentally, physically, and spiritually.

If there is no Heaven or hell, I have only improved my life here, helped other people, and built a good, respectable reputation. So, if you are right, it has cost me nothing. But if I am right and you are wrong, then you are in deep spiritual trouble. If hell and the devil are only fantasy, then you have had a nice laugh and I have had a nice life."

"But if the devil and hell are real," I said, "then you are in deep trouble." He asked me why, and I told him, "Because you are not born again." Jesus said that He is the only way. You must be born again to enter the Kingdom of Heaven. I taught him how (believe in your heart as Romans 10:9-10 says and confess with your mouth that Jesus is your Lord). This is being born again or born of the Spirit of God. It is so hard for me to believe that thousands will go to hell because they cannot (or perhaps will not) do these two easy, simple acts.

Let's look some more at Luke 16:23. We can answer

some questions and solve your problems. We learn here that the rich man lifted up his eyes. Verse 24 tells us that he wanted a drop of water from Lazarus' finger to be put on his tongue. Oh how he must have been in thirst! This is proof enough to me that those in hell have bodies of some sort. They have eyes, fingers, a tongue, etc.—bodies.

The rich man was said to be in torment. You see, he had feelings, and the Bible says that he saw Lazarus. This means he must have had his recognition. He recognized Lazarus. "Well," some people say, "in hell this is part of their punishment—they are tormented by having to watch us in Heaven." If this is for hell only, then why did Abraham talk to him, remember with him, and explain to him? Let's look at some more.

Verse 24 says that he cried. He had a voice. He said, "Have mercy on me." He had reasoning. The major difference from those in hell and those in paradise is that those in paradise had peace, relaxation, a lack of thirst, a lack of torment, a lack of concern for lost loved ones, etc. In hell there were torments, horrible cryings, pleas for mercy, pleas for water (horrible thirst), torments in flame, etc. You see, according to verse 25, the man in hell could even remember.

Hell—what a horrible thing to look forward to. What sting death has in life without God. What victory the grave has over people without Christ in their life.

Some people blame God for their lifestyle. They say that if God wanted them changed, He wouldn't have created them to live this way. Some say that if God wants them changed, He could just do a miracle and forcefully change them. How sad.

Some actually blame God for making a hell to put people in. If they only knew that hell and the pit were made for satan and his demons and that no man has to go there. No man has to go there! Yes, some will go there because they will disobey the Scriptures and refuse redemption. The Bible tells us that the dead will rise, both great and small. Both sinner and saint will look upon God and be judged.

I so much thank God for His blessed assurance that I am saved through His Son. I want to die and let the angels carry me to Jesus. Please understand that I'm not being spooky. I know that if you die your body is, by all means, going to show it. You will look dead. You will have need for a grave to lay your body in. But I mean spiritually. I don't want to go to the pits. I want to go to Jesus at the right hand of the Father.

Please look back with me at Luke 16:27. It says here, "I pray thee therefore, father . . ." I pray thee . . ." Imagine a man in hell who is so tormented and so low that he prayed for a beggar to go to his family. While living on the earth this rich man probably told his brothers over and over not to have anything to do with that church bunch. I can almost hear him now: "Don't listen to them; they only want your money. They only want your time and your labors. They are nuts and don't really know how to have fun."

Isn't this what most of us said before our born-again experience? Now, in hell, he is crying out for his family. I tell you friend—ten seconds in hell and you will be a firm believer in hell! Ten seconds in hell and, just like the rich man, you'll be a firm believer in prayer. This rich man used to feed the beggar with crumbs from his table. He thought he had it made. Now in hell, he is praying that the beggar would let him lick the tip of his finger for moisture. Have you ever been thirsty? Not like this! I tell you, ten seconds in hell and you'll get a horrible concern for your loved ones. Why wait for hell? There is more, there is more, there is so much more for those who are in Christ Jesus.

# CHAPTER 4
# JESUS RAISING A DEAD MAN

*"And many of the Jews came to Martha and Mary, to comfort them concerning their brother.*

*Then Martha, as soon as she heard that Jesus was coming, went and met him: but Mary sat still in the house.*

*Then said Martha unto Jesus, Lord, if thou hadst been here, my brother had not died.*

*But, I know, that even now, whatsoever thou wilt ask of God, God will give it thee.*

*Jesus saith unto her, thy brother shall rise again.*

*Martha saith unto him, I know that he shall rise again in the resurrection at the last day.*

*Jesus said unto her, I am the resurrection, and the life: he that believeth in me, though he were dead, yet shall he live:*

*And whosoever liveth and believeth in me shall never die. Believest thou this?*

*She saith unto him, Yea, Lord: I believe that thou art the Christ, the Son of God, which should come into the world.*

*And when she had so said, she went her way, and called Mary her sister secretly, saying, The Master is come, and calleth for thee.*

*As soon as she heard that, she arose quickly, and came unto him.*

*Now Jesus was not yet come into the town, but was in that place where Martha met him.*

*The Jews then which were with her in the house, and comforted her, when they saw Mary, that she rose up hastily and went out, followed her, saying, she goeth unto the grave to weep there.*

*Then when Mary was come where Jesus was, and saw him, she fell down at his feet, saying unto him, Lord, if thou hadst been here, my brother had not died.*

*When Jesus therefore saw her weeping, and the Jews also weeping which came with her, he groaned in the spirit, and was troubled,*

*And said, Where have ye laid him? They said unto him, Lord, come and see.*

*Jesus wept.*

*Then said the Jews, Behold how he loved him!*

*And some of them said, Could not this man, which opened the eyes of the blind, have caused that even this man should not have died?*

*Jesus therefore again groaning in himself cometh to the grave. It was a cave, and a stone lay upon it.*

*Jesus said, Take ye away the stone. Martha, the sister of him that was dead, saith unto him, Lord, by this time he stinketh: for he hath been dead four days.*

*Jesus saith unto her, Said I not unto thee, that, if thou*

*wouldest believe, thou shouldest see the glory of God?*

*Then they took away the stone from the place where the dead was laid. And Jesus lifted up his eyes, and said, Father, I thank thee that thou hast heard me.*

*And I knew that thou hearest me always: but because of the people which stand by I said it, that they may believe that thou hast sent me.*

*And when he thus had spoken, he cried with a loud voice, Lazarus, come forth.*

*And he that was dead came forth, bound hand and foot with graveclothes: and his face was bound about with a napkin. Jesus saith unto them, Loose him, and let him go."*

John 11:19-44

In this passage of scripture we read about Lazarus being raised from the dead. We all shout about this and get excited because Jesus can raise the dead. We all talk about the resurrection power that did this mighty act. We all rejoice in it. Yet even with all of this Jesus wept. Why wasn't He dancing and rejoicing? Jesus wept! Why wasn't He so very thrilled to bring Lazarus back? Jesus wept! Why wasn't He laughing and bragging like we would? Jesus wept!

In verse 11 we see that Jesus called Lazarus His friend. If he was a friend to Jesus, then he probably wasn't in hell. "No, no," some would say. Many of us think Lazarus was only asleep. This is not so. He was physically dead according to this same chapter, verses 13 and 14. Jesus told His disciples that Lazarus was dead. The Bible says that Jesus wept. Was He sad to bring Lazarus back to life? Was He sad because he had died? Was He weeping out of joy? I believe Jesus wept because He saw the sting in death for all Lazarus' family, and He saw them doing nothing about it.

I believe Jesus wept because He was to raise Lazarus only for him to die physically again. You have to understand that this resurrection of Lazarus was a natural resurrection. Yes, it was Jesus who raised him. Yes, it was supernatural resurrection power that performed this miracle. Even so, it was still a life raised to die again. Lazarus was not raised into a heavenly glorified body. He was to die a natural death again.

Let's examine this and pick out the things that are good for us to know for our own lives. Look with me again at verses 21-24. These verses teach us how not to think. In fact, these three verses really show us how people think today. Here Jesus is on the scene of Lazarus' death. Martha is telling Jesus that if only He would have been there her brother would not have died. Isn't this just the way we think today? "Oh if I only could have been in the early Church in Acts when Jesus was here." Don't we have the tendency to always look on the past and want to be there?

Notice verse 24. Martha is replying to Jesus saying that in the future her brother would rise again. Here we go again! We also do this. We look to some great revival or some great rapture to help us along. It seems as though we are always being attracted to the future or remembering the past. Jesus was trying to tell Martha to pay attention to the now—today! Jesus is still doing this with His people. Look at today. We are living in the today. The power of God isn't only for the early Church. Jesus was trying to convince Martha of this. He was trying to tell her that Lazarus would be raised even today.

Let me explain a little more about Jesus weeping and about the sting of death. In this same chapter of John, verse 33, we can see that death was being handled improperly, and it grieved Jesus. "When Jesus therefore saw her weeping, and the Jews also weeping which came with her, he groaned in the spirit, and was troubled." You see, it grieved the heart of Jesus when they were carrying on like that about Lazarus. They should have turned him loose and let him go. They themselves were putting sting into their brother's death. They sorrowed instead of rejoicing, and it troubled Jesus.

Now I tell you that Jesus was not an emotional, unstable person. He was and is Lord! He was troubled because they couldn't understand the power of God for their day. Nor did they have knowledge of the beauty of paradise, which is why they acted carnally toward the matter. "Now you're being pretty cold, Brother Barclay." No I'm not! When you realize the truth about this matter, you'll see that it is your selfishness that wants your loved ones back. They are in a place (if they were born again) where nothing can hinder or harm them. There is no sickness, poverty, or tribulation there.

Remember now that we are not seeking the thoughts of man. We want Bible thoughts, not theology. The raising of Lazarus was natural, in that he was raised to a natural state in his body of flesh, blood, and bones. We see this more clearly in verse 44. Here John recorded the way Lazarus came forth:

> *"And he that was dead came forth, bound hand and foot with graveclothes: and his face was bound about with a napkin. Jesus saith unto them, Loose him, and let him go."*

> John 11:44

21

Can't you see that even though Jesus raised him, he came out of the tomb totally bound? Yes it was great faith and supernatural power, but he was still limited to his natural body and also to his grave clothes. Have you ever thought about how he came out of that grave with his feet bound? This was a natural resurrection from paradise to bondage. Oh yes, I'm sure that Martha was very happy when Lazarus came forth. I wonder about how Lazarus felt. I wonder what he thought. I wonder about the life he had to live from this moment on. Did Jesus do wrong by raising him from the dead?

No! Jesus displayed power as He was directed by the Father, and I'm sure He did right. The point we want to make is that there is a great difference between a natural resurrection and a supernatural one. I want you to see that we don't have to wonder or struggle over lost loved ones. It is gain to be with Jesus.

# CHAPTER 5
# JESUS' RESURRECTION

*"The first day of the week cometh Mary Magdalene early, when it was yet dark, unto the sepulchre, and seeth the stone taken away from the sepulchre.*

*Then she runneth, and cometh to Simon Peter, and to the other disciple, whom Jesus loved, and saith unto them, They have taken away the Lord out of the sepulchre, and we know not where they have laid him.*

*Peter therefore went forth, and that other disciple, and came to the sepulchre.*

*So they ran both together: and the other disciple did outrun Peter, and came first to the sepulchre.*

*And he stooping down, and looking in, saw the linen clothes lying; yet went he not in.*

*Then cometh Simon Peter following him, and went into the sepulchre, and seeth the linen clothes lie,*

*And the napkin, that was about his head, not lying with the linen clothes, but wrapped together in a place by itself."*

John 20:1-7

As we see here, this is a completely different situation

than the raising of Lazarus. When Mary came to Jesus' tomb, there wasn't even a body to be concerned with. Jesus was gone! He wasn't lying there bound with grave clothes. He was gone. As we read verse 5, we see that the linen clothes were still there in the tomb, but the Body of Jesus was gone. Verse 6 says that Simon Peter went into the tomb and saw the linen clothes lying there. Now look real closely at verse 7. The napkin that was wrapped around His head was not lying with the linen clothes, but it was wrapped in a place by itself.

This truly was a supernatural resurrection. Jesus was gone! His body was not there. He had been born again of the Spirit of God. He had been raised with a heavenly glorified body. He didn't come forth bound by grave clothes; He came forth without even disturbing His grave clothes. He was not bound by death. He was raised to glory. He was never to die again. He lives! Our Savior is not dead but alive! Praise God, no one had to loose Him from any bondage!

> *"The former treatise have I made, O Theophilus, of all that Jesus began both to do and teach,*
>
> *Until the day in which he was taken up, after that he through the Holy Ghost had given commandments unto the apostles whom he had chosen:*
>
> *To whom also he shewed himself alive after his passion by many infallible proofs, being seen of them forty days, and speaking of the things pertaining to the kingdom of God . . ."*

Acts 1:1-3

Notice that the Word of God says that He showed Himself alive with many infallible proofs. I can see how this was by far a much greater resurrection than that of

Lazarus. Jesus was truly alive and never destined to die again. Imagine a man coming back from the dead and being with you 40 days and teaching you about the things of the Kingdom of God—infallible proofs! Let's look at some more.

> *"And as they thus spake, Jesus himself stood in the midst of them, and saith unto them, Peace be unto you.*
>
> *But they were terrified and affrighted, and supposed that they had seen a spirit.*
>
> *And he said unto them, Why are ye troubled? and why do thoughts arise in your hearts?*
>
> *Behold my hands and my feet, that it is I myself: handle me, and see; for a spirit hath not flesh and bones, as ye see me have.*
>
> *And when he had thus spoken, he shewed them his hands and his feet.*
>
> *And while they yet believed not for joy, and wondered, he said unto them, Have ye here any meat?*
>
> *And they gave him a piece of a broiled fish, and of an honeycomb.*
>
> *And he took it, and did eat before them."*
>
> Luke 24:36-43

Verse 39 is enough to convince me. He told them to touch His hands and feet. He wanted them to look at the scars on His body from the tree. Then He made this real profound statement: "A spirit hath not flesh and bones, as ye see me have." You see, Jesus wasn't some spooky spiritual manifestation. He was the Son of the Living God. He was still in bodily form. They could see Him, and He still had flesh and bones. It was His blood that was missing.

Life for Jesus in this new glorified body was no longer in the blood. He had spilled His blood for the real (zoe) life. Now verse 41 will really mess up your old theology. Here we see that Jesus was supposedly hungry. He asked if they had any meat. They gave Him fish and honeycomb, and He ate them. This truly was a godly resurrection from the natural way of life and death into the supernatural way of life never to face death again. Praise God! He lives!

*"So also is the resurrection of the dead. It is sown in corruption; it is raised in incorruption;*

*It is sown in dishonour; it is raised in glory: it is sown in weakness; it is raised in power:*

*It is sown a natural body; it is raised a spiritual body. There is a natural body, and there is a spiritual body.*

*And so it is written, the first man Adam was made a living soul; the last Adam was made a quickening spirit.*

*Howbeit that was not first which is spiritual, but that which is natural; and afterward that which is spiritual.*

*The first man is of the earth, earthy; the second man is the Lord from heaven.*

*As is the earthy, such are they also that are earthy: and as is the heavenly, such are they also that are heavenly.*

*And as we have borne the image of the earthy, we shall also bear the image of the heavenly.*

*Now this I say, brethren, that flesh and blood cannot inherit the kingdom of God; neither doth corruption inherit incorruption.*

*Behold, I shew you a mystery; We shall not all sleep, but we shall all be changed,*

*In a moment, in the twinkling of an eye, at the last trump: for the trumpet shall sound, and the dead shall be raised incorruptible, and we shall be changed.*

*For this corruptible must put on incorruption, and this mortal must put on immortality.*

*So when this corruptible shall have put on incorruption, and this mortal shall have put on immortality, then shall be brought to pass the saying that is written, Death is swallowed up in victory."*

1 Corinthians15:42-54

# CHAPTER 6
# DEATH IS AS REAL AS LIFE

Everyone makes light of death and tries to cover it up and push it to the back of their mind, until someone close to them dies. Then they wonder what death is all about. Was this person born again? Where did they go? We look into the casket and see the body empty and void of life. Where, oh where, is the person we so much loved? "Only yesterday . . ." some say. "Raise him from the dead!" "Maybe he isn't with the dead. Perhaps he is with the living." You see, we have power to raise some from the dead. We shouldn't even try to raise them all. It's not in your power to raise anyone but in the power of the Risen Savior. If God wants to use you as a vessel, let Him. If He doesn't, be careful.

Face death now, in Jesus' name. Know where you are going if you were to die today. I know, some would say that was a bad confession. Well, bad confession or not—know where you are going! Prepare your heart to be received by Jesus. Don't be caught dead without proper qualification. Fight for your life as long as you can. Believe for those 70 years. Rebuke the spirit of death, and tell it to flee from you. Don't practice things that lead to death. Stand on and walk into the authority of the Word of God!

Fight for your life. Fight for the lives of all those who are under your authority or headship. Make the thief back down. Let Jesus rise in your hearts. He is Lord!

Remember—death is swallowed up in victory!

# CHAPTER 7
# PREPARING YOURSELF FOR
# YOUR DEPARTURE

Christians above all people should have a grip on life and death. Because of our relationship with Jesus and our knowledge of the Bible, we should have a thorough understanding of this subject and be well prepared.

We should prepare ourselves in several crucial areas of life—ourselves, our families, our estate, our last will, our insurance, and even our own funeral arrangements.

One must be responsible enough to assure that he or she covers all spheres of life—the physical, the soulful, and the spiritual.

The Bible says it is appointed onto man once to die. This is talking about natural death. Each of us must be ready to face physical death and an eternal state. We know it's coming sooner or later (later is much better), so why be afraid to deal with it and face it?

In my years of ministry, especially pastoring, I have watched people ransack their families by unprepared and sudden deaths. I say unprepared and sudden because even when they know a death is going to occur (diseased patients, etc.), they still look at it blindly.

Let me remind you here that I am for living as long as one can. Fight for every breath. Stand for your loved ones as long as you possibly can. But if they go, don't allow the devil to hurt your family or steal from you any more than he already has.

To lose a loved one is painful and many times unfair. To not only lose the loved one but also everything they worked for and everything sentimental to you, is a royal rip-off. Why go broke burying your loved one when the insurance company could have paid for it or you could have done it long ago?

No, this is not a lack of faith or asking death to oblige you. Whom do you think the devil would want to strike the most—a family believing God with no protection (so that when the loved one dies the family is left desolate) or a family left rich and cared for? You know the answer. The devil's part of all this will be lessened by your wisdom and preparations. The last thing he wants is to leave your spouse as a rich widow who will feed the gospel and fund the destruction of Satan's work.

## PREPARE SPIRITUALLY

Give no place to the devil. Get your house in order. Protect your family.

I recommend that you have a long discussion with your spouse about what to do if you departed before her (or him), God forbid.

Have a strong Bible study and discussion with your children about life after death and death after death. Teach them about Heaven and our new life there.

Prepare yourself for eternity. Don't take for granted that a decision or commitment that you made a long time ago is still active today. Live each day as though it were your first day as a born-again Christian. Be born again, and live according to the Scriptures. Walk by faith, and be a true worshiper.

If you are not a born-again Christian, turn to the back of this book and pray the prayer that is there. Then seek out a Bible-preaching church, and ask the believers there for help so that you can grow as a Christian.

Fix any ill feelings or unforgivness that may still be in your life. Live thereafter as a clean, forgiving, and tenderhearted follower of Jesus Christ.

Leave a spiritual inheritance to your loved ones.

## PREPARE SOULFULLY

Overcome the fear of death and the fear of facing it. Get your mind made up that God is not the killer; He is the life-giver. If you are a Christian, you have nothing at all to fear. You are to live a long life and then be with the Lord forevermore. If you are not a Christian, you should become one right now. Don't wait another minute longer.

Renew your mind by the Word of God on these issues. You cannot waste your life away in bondage and torment because you are afraid to face life or, worse yet, face death.

As you study the Bible and learn more about eternal life, the fear of the unknown goes away from you. Also, of course, knowing the Lord Jesus Christ personally gives you great courage.

## PREPARE PHYSICALLY

Go down to the funeral home and ask to talk to a director there. Be sure you find a born-again director if at all possible. These born-again Christian directors seem to have a much better grip on these things.

Ask to plan out your entire funeral including burial and the entire costs. This may seem sort of morbid to you now, but it will save your family a lot of grief if anything ever happens to you (God forbid).

Also be sure that you have life insurance with coverage enough to pay everything off and leave a healthy chunk for your family. Never leave your affairs in shambles or give place for the world to get what rightfully belongs to your loved ones. This is wisdom. See a lawyer, and fill out a will. He will also coach you on any other things you should do to protect your family.

There is much to say but little space to say it. I only want to help you face these things and be wise and not negligent. I put myself in agreement with you right now that you will live an extremely long and healthy life. The Lord bless you!

# A PRAYER FOR YOU

My prayer for you is:

*". . . grant unto thy servants, that with all boldness they may speak thy word,*

*By stretching forth thine hand to heal; and that signs and wonders may be done by the name of thy holy child Jesus."*

Acts 4:29-30

Heavenly Father, I beseech You in Jesus' name, that You would cause each of us to grow in the character of our being. Help us to be more pleasing to You than we ever have been. Help us to speak boldly, yet in season. Help us to tell the truth and be what You want us to be.

Dear Lord, please melt away our facades and help us to stop playing games. Help each of us to see the Kingdom of God as the priority and not our own kingdom.

We are going to have backbone, Lord, in our servant-hood to You and our witness to the world.

We love You, Lord. Thank You for answering this prayer, Sir!

# PRAYER OF SALVATION

YOU CAN BE SAVED FROM ETERNAL DAMNA-TION and get God's help now in this life. All you have to do is humble your heart, believe in Christ's work at Calvary for you, and pray the prayer below.

Dear Heavenly Father,

I know that I have sinned and fallen short of Your expectations of me. I have come to realize that I cannot run my own life. I do not want to continue the way I've been living, neither do I want to face an eternity of torment and damnation.

I know that the wages of sin is death, but I can be spared from this through the gift of the Lord Jesus Christ. I believe that He died for me, and I receive His provision now. I will not be ashamed of Him, and I will tell all my friends and family members that I have made this wonderful decision.

Dear Lord Jesus,

Come into my heart now and live in me and be my Savior, Master, and Lord. I will do my very best to chase after You and to learn Your ways by submitting to a pastor, reading my Bible, going to a church that preaches about You, and keeping sin out of my life.

I also ask You to give me the power to be healed from any sickness and disease and to deliver me from those things that have me bound.

I love You and thank You for having me, and I am eagerly looking forward to a long, beautiful relationship with You.

# Books by Mark T. Barclay

## Beware of Seducing Spirits
This is not a book on demonology. It is a book about the misbehavior of men and women and the seducing and deceiving spirits that influence them to do what they do. Brother Barclay exposes the most prominent seducing spirits of the last days.

## Beware of the Sin of Familiarity
This book is a scriptural study on the most devastating sin in the Body of Christ today. The truths in this book will make you aware of this excess familiarity and reveal to you some counterattacks.

## Building a Supernatural Church
A guide to pioneering, organizing, and establishing a new local church. This is a fast-reading, simple, instructional guide to leaders and helps people who are working together to build the Church.

## Charging the Year 2000
This book will remind you of the last-days' promises of God as well as alert you to the many snares and falsehoods with which satan will try to deceive and seduce last-days' believers. "A handbook for living in the '90s."

## Enduring Hardness
God has called His Church an army and the believers soldiers. It is mandatory that all Christians endure hardness as good soldiers of Jesus Christ. This book will help build more backbone in you.

## How to Avoid Shipwreck
A book of preventive medicine, helping people stay strong and full of faith. You will be strengthened by this book as you learn how to anchor your soul.

## How to Relate to Your Pastor
It is very important in these last days that God's people understand the office of pastor. As we put into practice these principles, the Church will grow in numbers and also increase its vision for the world.

## How to Always Reap a Harvest
In this book Brother Barclay explains the principles that make believers successful and fruitful. It shows you how to live a better life and become far more productive and enjoy a full harvest.

## Improving Your Performance
Every Christian everywhere needs to read this book. Even leaders will be challenged by this writing. It will help tremendously in the organization and unity of your ministry and working force.

## The Making of a Man of God
In this book you'll find some of the greatest, yet simplest, insights to becoming a man or woman of God and to launching your ministry with accuracy and credibility. The longevity of your ministry will be enhanced by the truths herein. You will learn the difference between being a convert, an epistle, a disciple, and a minister.

## Preachers of Righteousness
This is not a book for pulpiteers or reverends only but for all of us. It reveals the real ministry style of Jesus Christ and the sold-out commitment of His followers— the most powerful, awesome force on the face of the earth.

## The Real Truth About Tithing
This book is a thorough study of God's Word on tithing, which will fully inform believers how to tithe biblically and accurately. You will be armed with the truth, and your life will never be the same!

## The Remnant Church
God has always had a people and will always have a people. Brother Barclay speaks of the upcoming revival and how we can be those who are alive and remain when our Master returns.

## Sheep, Goats, Wolves
A scriptural yet practical explanation of human behavior in our local churches and how church leaders and members can deal with each other. You will especially enjoy the tests that are in the back of this book.

## Six Ways to Check Your Leadings
It seems that staying in the main flow of Jesus is one of the most difficult things for believers to do, and I'm including some preachers. Many people border on mysticism and a world of fantasy. God is not a goofy god. He doesn't intend for His people to be goofy either. This book reveals the six most valuable New Testament ways to live in accuracy and stay perfectly on course. This book is a must for living in the '90s.

## The Sin of Lawlessness
Lawlessness always challenges authority and ultimately is designed to hurt people. This book will convict those who are in lawlessness and warn those who could be future victims. It will help your life and straighten your walk with Him.

## Warring Mental Warfare
Every person is made up of body, soul, and spirit and fights battles on each of these three fronts. The war against your soul (made up of your mind, will, and emotions) is real and as lethal as spiritual and natural enemies. This book will help you identify, war against, and defeat the enemies of your soul. Learn to quit coping with depression, anxiety, fear, and other hurts and begin conquering them now!

## What About Death
This book deals with the enemy—death and how to overcome it. I also explain what the bible says about life after death. I have found that many people have no real bible knowledge on this subject and therefore are unsure about it all the days of their lives.

## Basic Christian Handbook (mini book)
This mini book is packed full of scriptures and basic information needed for a solid Christian foundation. It would make an inexpensive and effective tract and is a must for new converts. Many church workers are using it for altar counseling.

## The Captain's Mantle (mini book)
Something happened in the cave Adullum. Find out how 400 distressed, indebted, and discontented men came out of that cave as one of the most awesome armies in history.